Book of Daniel

Golden Nuggets & Gems!

Valentina Epps

New American Standard Bible
New American Standard NEW AMERICAN STANDARD
BIBLE Copyright (C) 1960, 1962, 1963, 1968, 1971, 1972, 1973,
1975, 1977,1995 by THE LOCKMAN FOUNDATION A
Corporation Not for Profit LA HABRA, CA All Rights
Reserved http://www.lockman.org

New American Standard Bible 1995
"Scripture quotations taken from the (NASB®) New American
Standard Bible®, Copyright © 1995, by The Lockman
Foundation. Used by permission. All rights reserved.
www.lockman.org"

Copyright © 1999 - 2022 GoDaddy Operating Company, LLC
Artwork, fonts, color pallets, shapes and tools provided by
GoDaddy Studio
ALAMOFIRE
Copyright (c) 2014-2022 Alamofire Software Foundation
(http://alamofire.org/)
ALAMOFIREIMAGE
Copyright (c) 2015-2018 Alamofire Software Foundation
(http://Alamofire.org/)
Copyright © 2022 Emoji Character images/set by Apple, Inc.

Copyright © 2023 Valentina Epps
Valentina Epps Ministries, LLC

ISBN: 979-8-9877020-1-7   ISBN: 979-8-9877020-2-4
ISBN: 979-8-9877020-0-0

Edited by: Zane Haderlie
Edited by: Nancy Fredericks

TABLE OF CONTENTS

1. Introduction 5
2. Content 9
3. Notes 78
4. Who do you say Jesus is? 81
5. Prayer of Salvation 93

Introduction

How to use this book.

This is an interactive book. 📖

First, read the Scripture. Then interact with the Scripture by reading the questions that are around the Scripture and look for clues, make lists, and apply what you have learned to your life.
The Word of God will come alive.

Some of the questions have answers that can be found directly from the text.
The questions are in a specific color, and sometimes the answers to the questions are matched to the same color within the Scriptures. Typically, a line, circle, or an arrow is usually paired with the same color as the question.

ENJOY! 😉

EXAMPLE:

It is best to read the Scripture first.

"But Daniel made up his mind that he would not defile himself..."

DANIEL 1:8

Familiarize yourself with the Scripture. You may even try to memorize it.

Following each presentation of Scripture in this book 📖, you will have the opportunity to interact with the text. As a result, you may be able to apply these truths to your daily life. 😀

Let's Begin!

Familiarize yourself with the Scripture by reading it.

"But Daniel made up his mind that he would not defile himself..."

DANIEL 1:8

What did Daniel do?

What does Daniel make up his mind about?

Daniel purposed in his ♥ heart

"But Daniel made up his mind that he would not defile himself..."

DANIEL 1:8

to make unclean, dirty, or corrupt

What about you? Have you made up your mind, have you purposed in your heart NOT to defile yourself with the things of this world?

12

Ask 🙏 God to help you in an area where you might be struggling with things of this world. 🌍

Dear God,

13

Observe the Word of God. →

What observations did you make?

"Daniel said, "Let the name of God be blessed forever and ever, For wisdom and power belong to Him."

DANIEL 2:20

What do you learn about God?

WHAT DOES DANIEL SAY ABOUT THE NAME OF GOD?

"Daniel said, "Let the name of God be blessed forever and ever, For wisdom and power belong to Him.""

DANIEL 2:20

Whom does wisdom & power belong to?

Oh let us Bless the Name of God Forever and Ever!

Why?

For Wisdom & Power belong to HIM.

"It is He who changes the times and the epochs;
He removes kings and establishes kings;
He gives wisdom to wise men
And knowledge to men of understanding."

DANIEL 2:21

What do you learn about God?

Who changes the times & epochs?

Who removes & establishes kings?

"It is **He** who changes the times and the **epochs**; **He** removes kings and establishes kings; **He** gives wisdom to wise men And knowledge to men of understanding."

ERA, AGE, DATE, SPAN

DANIEL 2:21

What does God give to wise men?

What does God give men with understanding?

Did you notice...
God gives wisdom to wise men?
Did you notice...
God gives knowledge to men of understanding?

Become familiar with the Scripture and observe it.

Is there anything God is showing you?

"It is He who reveals the profound and hidden things; He knows what is in the darkness, And the light dwells with Him."

DANIEL 2:22

What do you learn about God?

What does God reveal?

"It is **He** who reveals the profound and hidden things; **He** knows what is in the darkness, And the light dwells with **Him**."

Does God know what is in the darkness?

What dwells with God?

DANIEL 2:22

Has God ever revealed to you the hidden things in your life? We can't hide anything from Him. He knows what is in the darkness.

Maybe God is speaking to you about the hidden things in your life.
Did you know that God is faithful to forgive us.
When we ask Him to forgive us, we become children of **LIGHT**.

The light dwells with Him. Isn't it exciting to know that we can walk in light & dwell with God. 😃

Carefully study this Scripture.

"He said, "Look! I see four men loosed and walking about in the midst of the 🔥 fire without harm, and the appearance of the fourth is like a son of the gods!"

"Then Nebuchadnezzar came near to the door of the furnace of blazing 🔥 fire; he responded and said, "Shadrach, Meshach and Abed-nego, come out, you servants of the Most High God and come here!" Then Shadrach, Meshach and Abed-nego came out of the midst of the 🔥 fire."

DANIEL 3:25 & 26

He who? ⬇ Nebuchadnezzar.

"He said, "Look! I see four men loosed and walking about in the midst of the fire without harm, and the appearance of the fourth is like a son of the gods!"

DANIEL 3:25

Fill in the blank:
The appearance of the fourth person is like...

HOW DOES NEBUCHADNEZZAR REFER TO SHADRACH, MESHACH, AND ABED-NEGO? SERVANTS OF WHO?

"Then Nebuchadnezzar came near to the door of the furnace of blazing fire; he responded and said, "Shadrach, Meshach and Abed-nego, come out, you servants of the Most High God, and come here!" Then Shadrach, Meshach and Abed-nego came out of the midst of the fire."

DANIEL 3:26

Who did Nebuchadnezzar ask to come out furnace of blazing fire?

Food For Thought:
Why didn't he call out the 4th person in the furnace?

Read and review the Word of God.

What is God showing you?

"Nebuchadnezzar the king to all the peoples, nations, and men of every language that live in all the earth: "May your peace abound! It has seemed good to me to declare the signs and wonders which the Most High God has done for me. "How great are His signs And how mighty are His wonders! His kingdom is an everlasting kingdom And His dominion is from generation to generation."

DANIEL 4:1-3

What is Nebuchadnezzar declaring?

"Nebuchadnezzar the king to all the peoples, nations, and men of every language that live in all the earth:
"May your peace abound!
It has seemed
good to me to declare the signs and wonders which
the Most High God has done for me.
"How great are His signs
And how mighty are His wonders!
His kingdom is an everlasting kingdom
And His dominion is from generation to generation."

DANIEL 4:1-3

King Nebuchadnezzar said, It has seemed good to him to declare the signs and wonders which the Most High God has done for him.

What about you? When was the last time you declared what God has done for you? Now is your chance. Declare below ⬇ what God has done for you.

 **Take time to memorize the Scripture.**

Is there anything you noticed from this Scripture?

"Now I, Nebuchadnezzar, praise, exalt and honor the King of heaven, for all His works are true and His ways just, and He is able to humble those who walk in pride."

DANIEL 4:37

What does Nebuchadnezzar do? He praises, exalts, and honors who?

What 3 things does Nebuchadnezzar say about the King of heaven?

"Now I, Nebuchadnezzar, praise, exalt and honor the King of heaven, for all His works are true and His ways just, and He is able to humble those who walk in pride."

DANIEL 4:37

What is God able to do?

We can learn life lessons **2** different ways.
1 - we can learn by example
2 - we can learn by experience

What can we learn from Nebuchadnezzar?

Let us learn by his example and not by his experience

"Then they brought the gold vessels that had been taken out of the temple, the house of God which was in Jerusalem; and the king and his nobles, his wives, and his concubines drank out of them. They drank the wine and praised the gods of gold and silver, of bronze, iron, wood, and stone."

DANIEL 5:3-4

KING BELSHAZZAR GAVE ORDERS TO BRING THE GOLD AND SILVER VESSELS WHICH NEBUCHADNEZZAR HAD TAKEN OUT OF THE TEMPLE, THE HOUSE OF GOD, WHICH WAS IN JERUSALEM. THEN THE KING, HIS NOBLES, HIS WIVES, AND HIS CONCUBINES DRANK OUT OF THEM.

"Then they brought the gold vessels that had been taken out of the temple, the house of God which was in Jerusalem; and the king and his nobles, his wives, and his concubines drank out of them. They drank the wine and praised the gods of gold and silver, of bronze, iron, wood, and stone."

DANIEL 5:3-4

WHERE DID THESE GOLD VESSELS COME FROM? WHOM DID THESE VESSELS BELONG TO?

After the king and his nobles, his wives, and his concubines drank out of God's holy vessels, whom did they praise?

What do you think? Did Belshazzar treat God's vessels as Holy?

Belshazzar praised other gods with God's vessels. He treated God's vessels as unholy.

1 CORINTHIANS 6:19-20

"OR DO YOU NOT KNOW THAT YOUR BODY IS A TEMPLE OF THE HOLY SPIRIT WITHIN YOU, WHOM YOU HAVE FROM GOD, AND THAT YOU ARE NOT YOUR OWN? FOR YOU HAVE BEEN BOUGHT FOR A PRICE: THEREFORE GLORIFY GOD IN YOUR BODY."

Do you know that you are God's holy vessel and that you are bought with a price?

Do you praise God with your life? Or does your life praise the things of this world?

Slow down and observe this Scripture.

What did you observe?

"I issue a decree that in all the realm of my kingdom people are to tremble and fear before the God of Daniel;

For He is the living God and enduring forever,
And His kingdom is one which will not be destroyed,
And His dominion will be forever.
He rescues, saves, and performs signs and miracles
In heaven and on earth,
He who has also rescued Daniel from the power of the lions."

DANIEL 6:26-27

DARIUS THE MEDE

"I issue a decree that in all the realm of my kingdom people are to tremble and fear before the God of Daniel;

For He is the living God and enduring forever,
And His kingdom is one which will not be destroyed,
And His dominion will be forever.
He rescues, saves, and performs signs and miracles
In heaven and on earth,
He who has also rescued Daniel from the power of the lions."

DANIEL 6:26-27

Did you notice all these amazing truths about

He is the "LIVING" God.
He endures forever.
His kingdom will not be destroyed.
His dominion will be forever.
He rescues.
He saves.
He performs signs & miracles.
　　Where? In heaven and on earth. 🌍
He rescued Daniel from the power of the lions'.

Which one of these truths is ministering to you?
Share it with a friend.
Just remember…
If our God can rescue Daniel from the lions' den,
He can rescue YOU!

Read the text.
Memorize the text.
Observe the text.

"I kept looking
Until thrones were set up,
And the Ancient of Days took His seat;
His vesture was like white snow
And the hair of His head like pure wool.
His throne was ablaze with flames,
Its wheels were a burning fire."

DANIEL 7:9

What [4] things do you learn about the Ancient of Days?

Don't miss any details about the Ancient of Days.

"I kept looking
Until thrones were set up,
And the [1] Ancient of Days took His seat;
[2] His vesture was like white snow
And the [3] hair of His head like pure wool.
[4] His throne was ablaze with **flames**,
Its wheels were a burning **fire**."

DANIEL 7:9

What has flames 🔥 and wheels?

Did you notice what the Word of God says about the Ancient of Days throne?

How is the Ancient of Days throne described?

His throne was ablaze with flames, Its wheels were a burning fire.

Investigate the Word.

What did you learn from investigating this Scripture?

"A river of fire was flowing
And coming out from
before Him;
Thousands upon thousands
were attending Him,
And myriads upon myriads
were standing before Him;
The court sat,
And the books were opened."

DANIEL 7:10

Him who?
The Ancient of Days

"A river of fire was flowing
And coming out from
before Him;
Thousands upon thousands
were attending Him,
And myriads upon myriads
were standing before Him;
The court sat,
And the books were opened."

DANIEL 7:10

Countless or extremely great number

...the court sat and books were opened.

One day every man, woman, and child will stand before the Ancient of Days and books will be opened.

If you were to stand before the Ancient of Days and books were opened about you, what would be written about you, your life, and your choices?

Have you sinned against God?
Do you need to ask God to forgive you?
Ask Him today!

Take time to become familiar with the text.

"Then I lifted my eyes and looked, and behold, a ram which had two horns was standing in front of the canal. Now the two horns were long, but one was longer than the other, with the longer one coming up last."

DANIEL 8:3

What do you learn about the ram? How many horns does it have?

"Then I lifted my eyes and looked, and behold, a ram which had two horns was standing in front of the canal. Now the two horns were long, but one was longer than the other, with the longer one coming up last."

DANIEL 8:3

Do you have any idea who the ram is? Sometimes God will reveal it in His Word.

Let's see if God reveals who the ram is. Look at Daniel 8:20

Daniel 8:20 "The ram which you saw with the two horns represents the kings of Media and Persia."

So, what does the ram with the two horns represent? Yes, you are correct, if you said...the kings of Media & Persia.

Did you notice that the ram was mentioned in verse 3 and 17 verses later the identity was revealed?

"When I, Daniel, had seen the vision, I sought to understand it;"

DANIEL 8:15

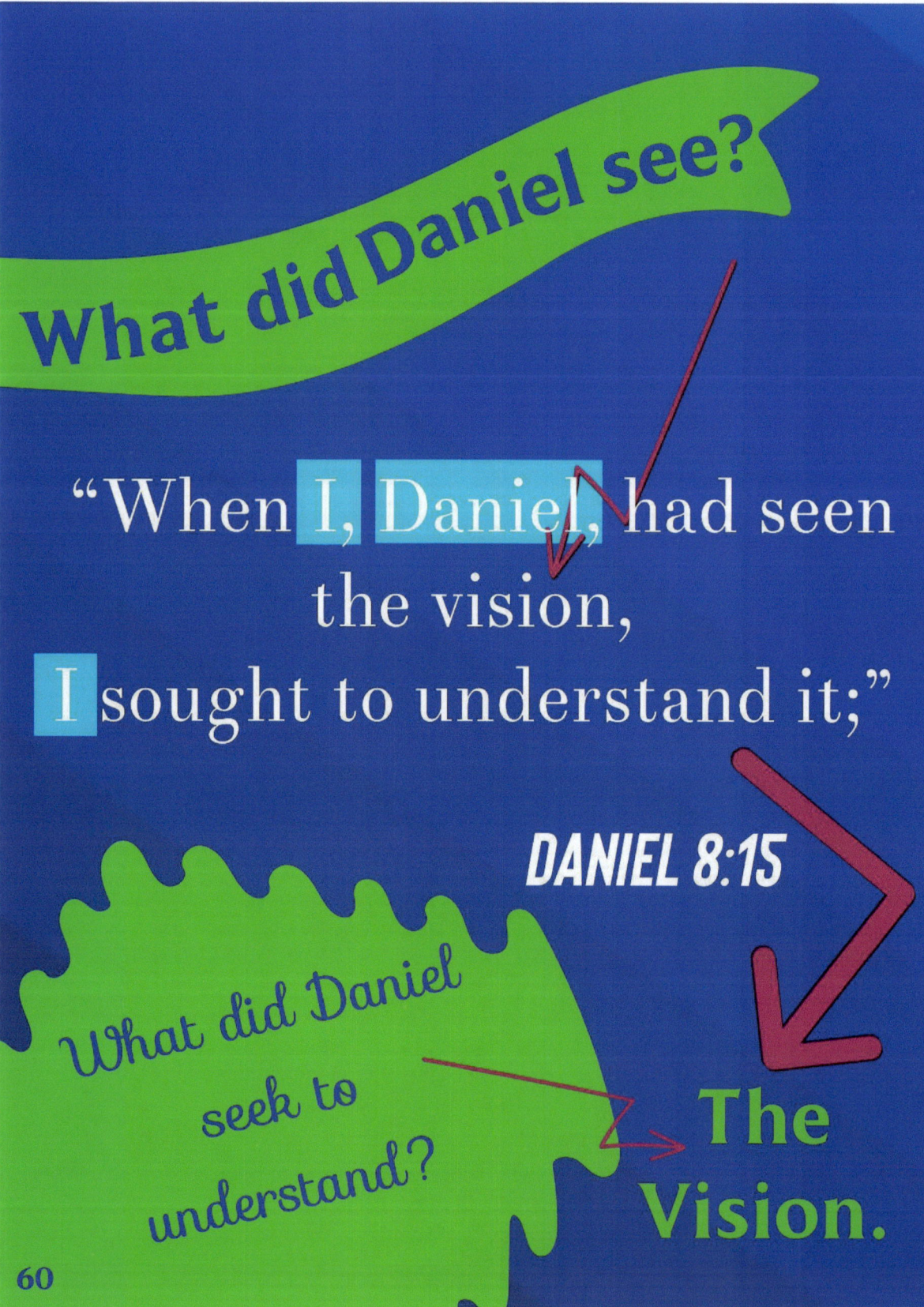

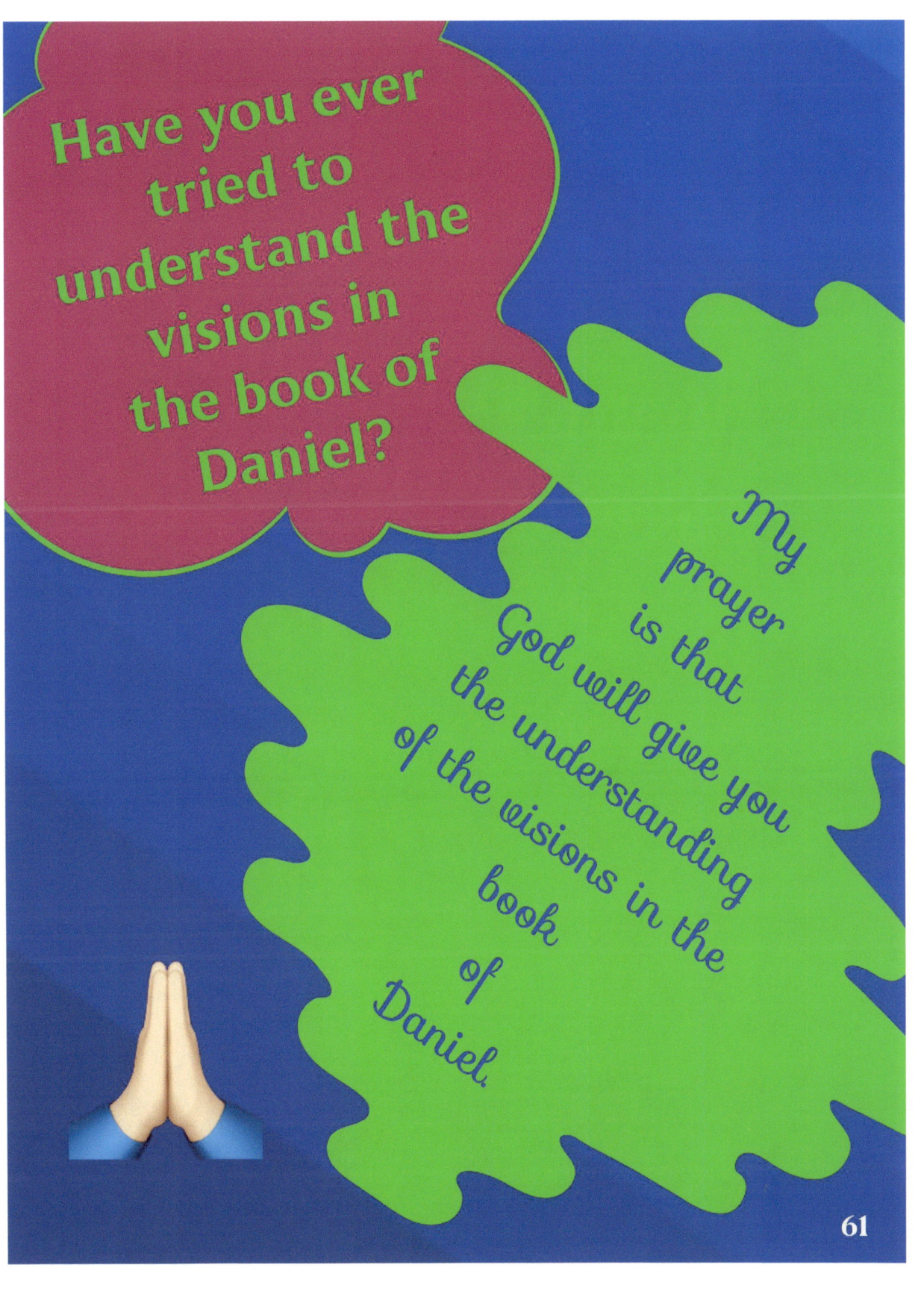

Read, study, and observe the text.

Did you observe anything interesting?

"Seventy weeks have been decreed
for your people and your holy city,
to finish the transgression,
to make an end of sin,
to make atonement for iniquity,
to bring in everlasting righteousness,
to seal up vision and prophecy and to
anoint the most holy place."

DANIEL 9:24

HOW MANY WEEKS HAVE BEEN DECREED?

WHO AND WHAT ARE THE 70 WEEKS DECREED FOR?

"Seventy weeks have been decreed for your people and your holy city, to finish the transgression, to make an end of sin, to make atonement for iniquity, to bring in everlasting righteousness, to seal up vision and prophecy and to anoint the most holy place."

DANIEL 9:24

What else do learn from verse 24? (Sometimes making a list will provide clarity.)

- to finish the transgression,
- to make an end of sin,
- to make atonement for iniquity,
- to bring in everlasting righteousness,
- to seal up vision and prophecy and to anoint the most holy place.

Challenge:
Read Daniel 9:24-27
List any other things you learned about the 70 weeks.

Investigate the Word of God. Study it.

What did you learn from investigating the text?

"In the third year of Cyrus king of Persia a message was revealed to Daniel, who was named Belteshazzar; and the message was true and one of great conflict, but he understood the message and had an understanding of the vision."

DANIEL 10:1

When did Daniel receive this vision?

What does Daniel understand?

"In the third year of Cyrus king of Persia a message was revealed to Daniel, who was named Belteshazzar; and the message was true and one of great conflict, but he understood the message and had an understanding of the vision."

DANIEL 10:1

What do you learn about the message? 1-2-3-4

Food for Thought

In Daniel 1:1

Daniel was taken to Babylon in the third year of the reign of Jehoiakim king of Judah.

In Daniel 10:1

Daniel was given a vision in the third year of the reign of Cyrus king of Persia.

**In Daniel chapter 1,
Daniel was approximately 15 years old.
(605 BC)
In Daniel chapter 10,
Daniel was approximately in his 80's.
(536 BC)**

Did you know that God can use you no matter how old you are?

Carefully study the Word of God. Investigate the Word of God.

Is there anything you noticed from this Scripture?

"but the people who know their God will display strength and take action."

DANIEL 11:32 b

Do we know our God?

"but the people who know their God will display strength and take action."

DANIEL 11:32 b

What will the people who know their God do?

The people who
know their God
will
display strength
and
take action

We are called to know our God.
We are called to display strength.
And we are called to take action.

What has God called you to do?

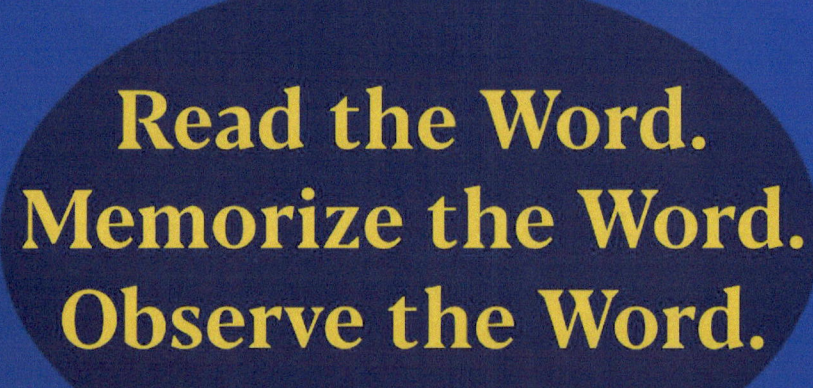

Read the Word.
Memorize the Word.
Observe the Word.

"Those who have insight will *shine* brightly like the brightness of the expanse of heaven, and those who lead the many to righteousness, like the stars forever and ever."

DANIEL 12:3

Do you shine brightly in a dark world?
I pray 🙏 that you will let your light shine before men, that they may see your good works, and glorify your Father which is in heaven.

"Those who have insight will **shine** brightly like the brightness of the expanse of heaven, and those who lead the many to righteousness, like the stars forever and ever."

DANIEL 12:3

Have you led anyone to righteousness?
It is my prayer 🙏 that you will not only lead ONE to righteousness, but that you will lead MANY to righteousness.

Those that have insight will do what?
They will **shine** brightly like the brightness of the expanse of heaven.

Let your light shine.

Are you leading many to righteousness?
Are you expanding heaven?

According to this Scripture, describe those who lead many to righteousness?

They Are Like The Stars Forever & Ever!

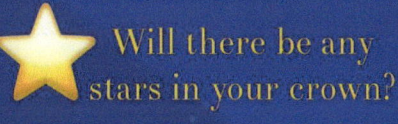
Will there be any stars in your crown?

The purpose of this section is for individuals to take a moment and talk to God. Ask God for guidance on how you may apply these truths to your life.

Small groups, Bible studies, and Sunday schools may use this section to record observations, truths, and discoveries.

Notes:

Who do you say Jesus is?

Who do you say Jesus is?

Where you spend eternity will depend on how you answer this question.

"In the beginning was the Word, and the Word was with God, and the Word was God. He was in the beginning with God. All things came into being through Him, and apart from Him nothing came into being that has come into being."

JOHN 1:1-3

Jesus is described as the Word.

What 6 things do you learn about the Word (Jesus)?

"In the beginning was the Word, and the Word was with God, and the Word was God. He was in the beginning with God. All things came into being through Him, and apart from Him nothing came into being that has come into being."

JOHN 1:1-3

Did you notice that Jesus is described as the Word? He was in the beginning, He was with God, and He is God. All things came into being through Jesus, and apart from Jesus, nothing came into being.

This includes YOU!

"In Him was life, and the life was the Light of men."

JOHN 1:4

What else do you learn about Jesus?

"In Him was life, and the life was the Light of men."

JOHN 1:4

In Jesus is life, and the life was the Light of men.

"He was in the world, and the world was made through Him, and the world did not know Him."

JOHN 1:10

How was the world made?

"**He** was in the world, and the world was made through **Him**, and the world did not know **Him**."

JOHN 1:10

Jesus was in the world, but did the world know Him?

Do you know Jesus?

"And the Word became flesh, and dwelt among us; and we saw His glory, glory as of the only Son from the Father, full of grace and truth."

JOHN 1:14

The Word (Jesus) became flesh and dwelt among us, and we saw His glory, glory as of the only begotten from the Father, full of grace & truth.

"And the Word became flesh, and dwelt among us; and we saw His glory, glory as of the only Son from the Father, full of grace and truth."

JOHN 1:14

Did you notice what this Scripture says about Jesus?

Jesus is full of Grace & Truth.

Do you need Grace?

Are you seeking Truth?

Call on Jesus.
Jesus is the answer!

→

Prayer of Salvation 🙏

Accepting Jesus Christ as your Savior, and Lord is one of the most important decisions you will make in your life.

Let this prayer be yours.

Prayer of Salvation

God,
I believe that Jesus died for my sins.
I believe that Jesus was buried and that He was raised on the third day.
I am a sinner and I ask that You would forgive me of all my sins. I confess my sins to You. Forgive me. Come into my heart, be Lord and Savior of my life. Thank you.
In Jesus' Name I pray, Amen.

I pray that you will find a good local church that is Bible believing and Spirit filled.
Who do you say Jesus is?
I hope you can say...

"He is my Savior and Lord!"

www.ingramcontent.com/pod-product-compliance
Lightning Source LLC
Chambersburg PA
CBHW042000150426
43194CB00002B/77